Contents

OFFICE FOR STANDARDS
IN EDUCATION

PROMOTING HIGH ACHIEVEMENT

FOR PUPILS WITH SPECIAL EDUCATIONAL NEEDS IN MAINSTREAM SCHOOLS

A report from the Office of Her Majesty's Chief Inspector of Schools

ISBN 0 11 350076 9

Office for Standards in Education
Alexandra House
29-33 Kingsway
London WC2B 6SE

Telephone 0171-421 6800

1 Background

The provision made for pupils with special educational needs (SEN) has been the focus of considerable change and development for many years. Most importantly, three major pieces of legislation in the form of the Education Acts of 1981, 1988 and 1993 have led local education authorities (LEAs) and schools to review their responsibilities for meeting the SEN of pupils. Following the implementation of the 1981 Education Act in 1983, pupils with more complex needs were assessed through a multidisciplinary procedure leading to a formal statement of their needs. A wider group of pupils with SEN was identified and a variety of strategies developed to support them in mainstream classes. The 1988 Act, with the introduction of Local Management of Schools (LMS), gave increased responsibilities for provision at school level with the delegation of funding from the LEA. Ultimately the 1993 Act, with the associated guidance in the form of the Code of Practice[1] further increased the responsibilities of schools to specify the type and levels of support offered for pupils with SEN, whether they have a statement of SEN or not.

The inspection evidence for this survey was undertaken between March and December 1994 and coincided with the gradual implementation by schools of the guidance contained within the draft Code of Practice. Evidence suggests that the group of pupils with SEN but without a statement, were increasingly being identified according to the staged approach described in the Code of Practice.

[1]*The Code of Practice on the identification and assessment of special educational needs.* (DFE,1994). A separate report on the implementation and effectiveness of the Code of Practice resulting from a survey undertaken by HMI during the period September 1994-December 1995 will be published early in 1996.

'Special educational needs' is a broad term intended to include pupils with learning difficulties arising from an intellectual, sensory, physical or emotional disability.

The use of this term by LEAs and schools in the survey was applied unevenly across the country and has given rise to the identification of widely differing populations.

For the purpose of this report the term 'special educational needs' refers to all pupils who are considered by schools to have a SEN, whether they have a statement or not. In 1995, figures published by the Department for Education and Employment (DFEE) indicated that 54 per cent of all pupils with a statement of SEN were being taught in mainstream schools. This figure reflects, among other things, the significant change in provision for such pupils over the last few years. Whilst the findings of the Warnock Report (1978) suggested that as many as 1 in 5 children (20 per cent) were likely to experience learning difficulties at some stage in their school career and 1 in 6 children (18 per cent) at any one time, inspection evidence from this survey suggests that this figure can vary from as little as 1.5 to 53 per cent, depending on the identification procedures used by a school and LEA.

2 The Survey

The objectives for this national survey were:

- to determine how LEAs and schools identified pupils with SEN;
- the provision made for the pupils;
- an evaluation of the achievement of these pupils in mainstream schools.

Visits were made by HMI across 33 LEAs to:

- learning support services (LSS)[2];
- LEA officers/inspectors for SEN;
- 38 secondary schools and middle (deemed secondary);
- 105 primary and first schools;
- 785 lessons which included whole class or groups withdrawn from a class.

Wherever possible visits were made to secondary schools and the associated primary schools which contributed the majority of their pupils.

Many of the lessons observed involved pupils with statements. However, the major focus was on the much larger group of pupils with SEN but without a statement. Discussions were also held with teachers, pupils, parents and governors. The majority of pupils observed had access to the full range of National Curriculum subjects.

The key areas for investigation at school and LEA level were:

- assessment and identification of SEN;
- policies and guidance for SEN;

[2]This description covers the wide range of support services and includes learning, behaviour and sensory services.

- structures, deployment of resources and monitoring of SEN;
- staff development for SEN;
- progress and achievement by all the pupils identified by the schools as having SEN.

Judgements about pupils' attainments were not made on the basis of age-related expectations but on the basis of inspectors' judgements of whether pupils were making sufficient progress in relation to their ability. In order to make these judgements, information about pupils' levels of attainment was obtained from statements, annual reviews, reports, discussion with teachers and pupils andscrutiny of work over a period of time.

Attempts were made to assess the progress of all the pupils with SEN in the classes visited, and to compare this with the achievement of the other pupils. However, the major focus of the exercise was those pupils who are now likely to be on the school's SEN Register at Stages 1, 2 or 3 of the Code of Practice. In some classes this was just one pupil, in others over half of the class; usually there was a group of 4-6 pupils in a class.

The organisation of special needs provision in schools varied considerably. In some schools extra help was provided within mainstream classes. In others it was largely by the withdrawal of individuals or small groups. In most schools it was a successful combination of in-class support and withdrawal. Visits were also made to classes where there was no additional support, in order to judge standards of achievement and the quality of provision for pupils with SEN.

3 Main Findings

Progress and achievement

The survey found that:

- the overall standards achieved by pupils with SEN are generally sound, though in the nursery, and at Key Stage 1 and Key Stage 2 standards are better than at Key Stage 3 and Key Stage 4;
- in the nursery, and at Key Stage 1 and Key Stage 2, all pupils gain from extra in-class support, but pupils with SEN gain most. In Key Stage 3 and Key Stage 4 with few exceptions, the same effect was only apparent where the support was provided by a teacher;
- where support is not available, or where it is insufficiently well-informed, both the standards of achievement and the quality of education suffer;
- where no extra support is present, pupils with SEN benefit no less than others from good teaching, which takes full account of the needs of all pupils;
- at all key stages the most influential factor on the effectiveness of in-class support is the quality of joint planning of the work between class/subject teacher and the support teacher or special support assistant (SSA);
- SSAs are effective in helping to raise standards at primary phase, but markedly less so at secondary phase;
- at all key stages the quality of teaching and learning and the standards achieved by pupils with SEN are frequently too variable both within and between schools;
- the quality of educational provision in withdrawal sessions work with small groups or individuals outside the classroom is generally sound, but raises pupils' standards more at secondary level than at primary.

School provision - policy and practice

- most schools are reviewing their policies for SEN. These reviews generally provide clearer information and guidance on administrative and organisational issues; however, practical guidance on strategies to implement and evaluate policy is not always included;
- there is a wide variation between schools across and within LEAs in the numbers of pupils identified as having SEN. Identification and assessment procedures are too inconsistent;
- as the survey progressed, the Code of Practice had an increasing influence on the schools. Most of the schools visited later in the survey period had developed a greater consistency in the way pupils were identified at Stages 1-3 of the Code of Practice;
- insufficient support by the senior management team (SMT) for SEN co-ordinators (SENCOs) in secondary schools, and a lack of time for SENCOs in primary schools are two prominent factors which constrained the effective co-ordination of provision across a school;
- in the earlier stages of the survey, many schools had an inaccurate knowledge of the exact level of resourcing for pupils with SEN. Towards the end of the survey, schools became more aware of the delegated funding available for special educational needs, and this strengthened their monitoring of the provision available.

LEA provision - policy and practice

- policies and guidance on SEN are in place in most LEAs. The majority provide appropriate information and many are being reviewed in the light of the Code of Practice;
- the majority of LEAs have experienced major reorganisation(s) of SEN provision over a period of three years and this has adversely affected the quality of monitoring,

which is unsatisfactory in most LEAs;

- fewer than half the LEAs visited have the necessary procedures for allocating resources to schools;
- LEAs continue to provide in-service education training (INSET) for schools. Much of the recent training aims to raise awareness of the Code of Practice but there has been little practical guidance about how to teach SEN pupils more effectively;
- less than half the LEAs provide appropriate training for their learning support services staff.

4 Progress and Achievement

Pupils with SEN in classes with no additional teacher or SSA support.

The total number of lessons seen without additional support was 223 (5 nursery, 145 primary, 73 secondary). This represents 28 per cent of all lessons in the survey. Overall achievement for pupils without SEN is judged to be sound in 82 per cent of lessons at Key Stages 1, 71 per cent at Key Stages 2, and 75 per cent at Key Stages 3/4. For pupils with SEN the figures were 67 per cent, 63 per cent and 58 per cent respectively. In general the quality of teaching and learning has major shortcomings for pupils with SEN in too many lessons. Nevertheless, the teaching in a few lessons demonstrate some good features in addition to those which characterise all teaching of quality. These include high but realistic expectations, the ability to explain things clearly and use questions effectively, specific learning objectives and good classroom management. The qualities that lifted these lessons above the others include:

- careful planning that takes account of the needs of all pupils;
- strategic help, with the teacher targeting tasks to those

individuals who require more teaching help;

- work that is appropriately matched to individual need and taught using a range of different pupil groupings, tasks or resources;
- good procedures for assessment and recording.

Examples of good practice in classes without additional support

In this class of Year 3 and Year 4 pupils, 13 of the 35 are on the SEN register. Three different levels of work have been produced for both maths and English activities. Those pupils without SEN are working at National Curriculum Levels 3 and 4. All groups are being challenged appropriately: an able group by a tessellation activity; a middle group is learning to understand symmetry by the use of mirrors and reflection; and a less able group is learning to recognise and match 2D shapes with real objects. A group of fluent readers sequences the events of a story while less able readers arrange simple sentences or captioned pictures in the correct order. The quality of relationships in the class is excellent and all the children are clearly enjoying the work and experiencing a sense of achievement. They all show good, independent work skills and manage the learning resources well. All are making clear progress at levels appropriate to their ability. The organisation of the teaching is first class and operates at a range of levels including: good room layout; accurately chosen yet flexible groupings; easy access to resources which promotes pupil independence and allows the teacher more time to teach rather than supervise activities. In addition, targeted and focused teaching, planned on a weekly basis, allows all pupils balanced opportunities for peer learning, individual work and teacher support. All this is underpinned by good recording of pupils' work, with records well-used for future planning and excellent liaison between the class teacher and SENCO.

In a music lesson, 22 Year 8 pupils are learning about African drumming as part of their work on complex rhythms and how to build them up. The lesson incorporated learning about notation, syncopation and performance. Pupils are grouped around tables with a very wide range of instruments, enough for everyone. Gradually, under the teacher's instructions, pupils build up a series of complex rhythms. In the next lesson they will create their own.

The entire session is a superb achievement for all pupils. Pupils listen intently (the silence between the bursts of sound is profound), offer comment when appropriate, respond on cue and write down their own contributions to the piece being created collectively. A wide range of musical signs and terms is well understood by the majority of the class and some handle notation confidently. The pupils show intense concentration and a desire to get it right.

One child in this group is undergoing a Stage 4 assessment, his literacy and numeracy skills are weak and he finds sustained concentration difficult. However, in this session his knowledge and love of music are used to great effect by the teacher. He is rewarded with praise and gains in skill and understanding. All pupils take part and are appropriately challenged by the teacher who varies the complexity of the rhythm demanded, taking account of prior learning. A skilful teacher whose explanations help understanding the building up a complex rhythm is likened to the 'layering of a sandwich', syncopation is described successfully as 'playing across the beat'. Teacher demonstrations are clear and continue to challenge pupils beyond the lesson. ("Find the name and country of origin of an unusual instrument by the end of the day".) Not a minute is wasted in this lesson, yet it is full of humour and enjoyment. Pupils are reluctant to stop for lunch and want to talk about other recent musical achievements.

Pupils with SEN in classes with additional teacher or SSA support.

The total number of lessons with additional support was 333. This represents 43 per cent of all lessons seen during the survey (27 per cent with teacher support, compared with 16 per cent SSA). Overall achievement for pupils without SEN is judged to be sound in 83 per cent of lessons at Key Stages 1, 81 per cent of lessons at Key Stages 2 and 68 per cent of lessons at Key Stages 3/4. For pupils with SEN the figures were 83 per cent, 85 per cent, and 47 per cent of lessons respectively. There is less SSA support at secondary than at primary level, while the amount of teacher support increases across the key stages.

At these levels and with few exceptions only teacher support made a positive impact on standards of achievement. In particular, where it was possible to identify qualified SEN support, effective partnerships between class and support teachers often resulted in changes of overall teaching strategy that benefited a wider range of children.

Successful SSA support is invariably linked to good INSET opportunities, clear guidance and close oversight of the work by the class teacher, the SENCO or in many cases at primary level, the head or deputy of the school. SSA support is markedly more effective at primary level perhaps because liaison between class and support assistants is easier when fewer adults are involved. By Key Stages 3 and 4 a greater range of skilled specialist intervention is required to raise pupils' achievements. However, the quality of support given by SSAs to pupils with physical impairment is generally good at both primary and secondary level. In many cases an excellent relationship had built up between the SSA and the pupil over a period of time, enabling the pupil to be well integrated and successful with the mainstream work.

It is difficult for a support teacher or SSA to work effectively in a poorly managed class, although occasionally examples of skilful support teaching in a class can act as a model or catalyst for a weak teacher. It is undoubtedly the case that an experienced and trained support teacher (and on occasion an SSA) make a significant difference in a class that is difficult to control.

The key features of lessons in which high quality provision is made using in-class support for pupils with SEN are:

- good team working between support staff and class teacher; ie joint planning to allow pupils with SEN to work on the same curriculum area or theme as the rest of the class, but at an appropriate level;
- the support teacher or SSA being well supplied with information about the work to be attempted;
- the support teacher introducing additional materials and strategies to enable pupils with SEN to take part often these are of use to a wider group of pupils;
- the support teachers or SSA working, for example, with a more able group, enabling class teacher to focus on those pupils who need more help;
- ensuring that pupils of all abilities are adequately challenged to solve problems, reflect, formulate strategies, and act independently; ie it is not helpful to the pupil if the support teacher or SSA largely does the work for the child;
- ensuring the integration of pupils with SEN into the whole class.

Examples of good practice in classes with additional teacher or SSA support

The 27 pupils in this Year 4 class have just returned from a school trip to Devon and are diligently completing their project books about the visit. The work involves mostly English and geography (local and contrasting areas) and is of a good standard in relation to pupils' capabilities. Pupils are keen to talk about the visit which was obviously a rewarding experience.

A child with a statement, previously in the school's Emotional Behavioural Difficulties Unit, is being integrated into the mainstream class before transfer to middle school. He is reworking his brief description of the visit with the help of an SSA. His statement is for speech and language difficulties compounded with behaviour problems. His literacy skills were very weak but he is now making good progress. He has difficulty with spelling so the SSA encourages him to build difficult words with alphabet letter shapes before writing them in his book. On occasion she directs him to hunt for words in a dictionary. The pupil concentrates hard and clearly benefits from the sensitive support offered. He is gently but firmly kept on task and prompted at appropriate points to become a more independent learner.

The new topic in this geography lesson for Year 7 pupils is 'Italy'. Three boys, one of whom is also bi-lingual, need support. The teacher starts by asking the boys to share what they know about Italy. Somewhat predictably they venture: good football teams; pizza; the mafia; pasta; ice cream and the Romans! They are then asked to jot down what they know under the following headings: sport, food, cities, music, buildings. This is followed by a range of different tasks: two able boys are asked to research questions about Italy that they will subsequently pose to the teacher and the rest of the class; some are given a comprehension task of completing a passage with vocabulary help offered; others are told to carry out the task but to use their own words and expand the information by using reference books. The pupils settle quickly and work with enthusiasm, many displaying good study skills (using atlases and dictionaries, note-taking). The boys with SEN take a full part in the lesson and make good progress helped unobtrusively by the support teacher who has been involved with the preparation of the resources. A well planned and managed lesson - excellent match of task to individual or group need so that all are working on the same content/theme. The least able are helped by the carefully structured tasks and the most able challenged by the more open-ended activities. Both teachers say they have learnt from each other.

Pupils with SEN who are withdrawn from their mainstream class for individual or group work.

A total of 229 withdrawal lessons or sessions was seen (153 at primary and 76 at secondary level). This represents 29 per cent of the sample. Many of those seen at Key Stages 1 were Reading Recovery sessions (RR). These were frequently of a good quality, reflecting the intensive training given to RR tutors. Most withdrawal sessions at all key stages are taken by qualified teachers, often members of the LEA LSS; others are taken by SSAs. Achievement in approximately 80 per cent of the lessons is sound or better; the quality of teaching and learning is also good in a high proportion of the sessions. However, there is a marked difference in the quality of provision between those sessions led by qualified teaching staff and those taken by SSAs. At Key Stages 1, for example, the quality of teaching and learning is judged sound or better in 90 per cent of the periods taken by qualified teaching staff, but in only 67 per cent of those taken by SSAs. The majority of sessions are concerned with improving literacy. Schools rarely take a broader view of SEN to include basic numeracy or a range of practical skills.

The key features of lessons in which high quality provision is made using withdrawal group/individual support are:

- clearly targeted, focused and challenging activities;
- where there is a small group, careful planning which responds to the range and specific nature of the child's individual learning needs;

- tracking of individual progress against carefully constructed programmes of work;
- sessions linked to main class work, the class teacher aware of what takes place and the sharing of records which helps planning;
- teaching which fits into whole-school approaches so that if a reading session concentrates on tightly focused phonic skills, attention is also given to reading for meaning;
- flexible use of time so that pupils did not lose their curricular entitlement (for example, not always being taken out of French and becoming a failure at that too).

Examples of good practice where pupils are withdrawn from mainstream classes for individual or group work

A counselling session for a young visually impaired Year 2 boy with an SSA and class teacher resulted from a series of conflicts with other pupils. In a quiet room the adults and child look at toys and talk about them before moving on to discuss his unacceptable behaviour. Sensitive, firm and constructive comments are followed by the setting of realistic targets for the rest of the day. The successful achievement in the improvement of behaviour resulted in the award of a sticker for good work and words of encouragement from the head teacher. A judicious and timely whole - school response to a special need, consistent with the school's pastoral care policy.

Ten pupils are withdrawn from two classes at Year 3/Year 4 as they have similar literacy difficulties (NC Level 2 reading and writing, below age-related expectations). The focus is on reading for meaning, writing and spelling, with the specific aim of developing levels of concentration. The work is linked to 'Billy the Bothersome Bully' as part of a whole school anti-bullying focus. The planning and organisation of the session by the class and support teachers shows a thorough understanding of pupils' individual needs - a range of appropriate worksheets, carefully selected, supports reading and writing activities, and IT software, with a voice synthesizer, encourages independent learning. The pupils enjoy these thrice weekly sessions, can articulate why they need extra help, but display good levels of self esteem. They apply previously learnt skills to the new words and sentences. Progress is clear, carefully monitored and conveyed to class teachers. Resources are varied and stimulating and record keeping is excellent. A Year 10 student has a statement for specific learning difficulties and is receiving one-to-one English support in the base for SEN. Normally he receives in-class support but today his tuition tutor (from the central LSS team) wants to play him part of a tape recording of the Shakespeare play being studied by the whole class. They all have to write an essay on 'Brutus as a tragic hero'. It is less distracting for the pupil here to hear the tape in the base for SEN and for the teacher to draw attention to specific aspects of the play. In this session the pupil listens well and is able to pick out the quotations he needs to support his arguments in the essay. He discusses the meaning of words such as 'virtuous' and 'defect', and is successful in identifying those aspects of Brutus's behaviour that indicate flaws in his character. He is very appreciative of the help as he has missed a few lessons and is very keen to catch up. The nature of the support has been negotiated between the support and class teacher - the taped recording being thought particularly useful. It helps him understand the play. The support teacher guides the pupil in the planning and marshalling of the evidence for his essay. He has great problems with writing but produces good standards of achievement in relation to ability with this support.

5 School Provision

Policies and guidance, including identification and assessment

The features of a good policy and associated guidance for schools are clearly articulated within the Code of Practice.

The majority of schools at the time of the survey were in the process of reviewing their policies in the light of the Code. Whilst considerable progress is being made to upgrade and make school policies more precise and helpful, initially the main thrust in most schools gave priority to procedural and administrative detail. Less than half the survey schools provided appropriate guidance for class or subject teachers on strategies for teaching and learning for the range of pupils with SEN.

There continues to be wide variation between schools across and within LEAs, in the numbers of pupils identified as having SEN. In almost all cases, where figures are available the schools identify a much larger proportion than the LEAs. One LEA reported 8 per cent of pupils with SEN, but an average of the schools inspected in the same LEA reported 26 per cent. In the few LEAs that gave clear criteria and guidance for identification and assessment, there was greater consistency between the primary and secondary schools' identification arrangements. In these schools a more accurate assessment of need, leading to targeted support, more effective teaching and learning, and better use of resources was evident.

The good identification and assessment arrangements, in just over half the schools, put emphasis on detailed observation of pupils with SEN. On some occasions this was facilitated by the SENCO teaching the class, thereby allowing the class teacher to make detailed observations of the work of pupils with SEN whilst an activity was undertaken. Discussion between the SENCO and the teacher could then be informed by what was actually happening, so that the specialist support was more precisely targeted and hence more effective in raising standards.

The key features of school policies and guidance which are most successful in promoting high achievement for pupils with SEN are:

- a commitment to SEN provision that permeates the

whole organisation of a school;

- recognition of SEN within all other school policies and documentation, especially the School Development Plan (SDP);
- an explanation of the principles, statutory requirements, LEA policy and other influences on which the policy is based;
- identifying the groups on whom the policy is targeted - class teachers, specialist support teachers, parents, other professionals;
- practical strategies for identification and assessment of pupils' short, medium and long-term learning difficulties, with clear expectations and advice for staff on writing individual education plans (IEPs);
- teaching and learning strategies which include how to observe pupils and modify teaching accordingly;
- approaches to be taken when reporting to parents;
- arrangements for ensuring the effective transfer of records when pupils move to the next stage of education (or to other schools);
- specific strategies for monitoring and evaluating the success of the policy and guidance.

The key features of effective assessment strategies that more accurately identify pupils with SEN are:

- teacher observation using formal and informal strategies;
- teacher assessments of progress within National Curriculum Levels;
- pupils' assessment of their own progress;
- appropriately chosen diagnostic standardised assessments;

- parental evidence;
- statutory end of key stage assessments.

Structures and deployment of resources

The majority of schools surveyed have an identifiable SENCO and some schools designate the role as a Learning Support or Curriculum Support co-ordinator. Where the identified co-ordinator is supported by a designated person with senior management responsibility the curricular and pastoral provision for pupils with SEN is considerably more effective in meeting their needs and raising achievement. The most effective management structures in both primary and secondary schools are those which are based on clear lines of responsibilities for SEN, where class or subject teachers are expected to take the responsibility for the pastoral and academic care of all pupils - including those with SEN.

Secondary schools

In almost all secondary schools there is a designated SENCO with the senior management team (SMT) having oversight in the majority of schools.

Usually, however, the day to day organisation and administration is the responsibility of the SENCO with SMT responsibilities existing in name only. Too often the SENCOs reported that they were unsupported by senior management.

In less than half of schools do the organisational arrangements allow the SENCO to plan and target support effectively. More usually timetabling arrangements do not prioritise support for pupils with SEN. As a consequence, pupils can be helped in class by teachers with little subject specialist knowledge who then fulfil a supervisory role to pupils rather than teach them. Sometimes teachers of SEN support a subject area they are not qualified in and the need for joint planning is more imperative.

Primary schools

Almost all primary schools have a designated SENCO and in over half of schools this is either the head or deputy headteacher. The best practice which promotes achievements for pupils with SEN is found when the SENCO has sufficient time to liaise, co-ordinate and support staff in school; usually in excess of one day a week. This occurs in approximately one-third of the schools and a variety of ways are found to facilitate this. Most commonly, headteachers release time for the SENCO by teaching themselves or targeting resources for supply cover to enable the SENCO to support in class and fulfil a co-ordination role. An effective strategy found in six large primary schools in different LEAs is to give SENCOs no class responsibility and programme a system of team- teaching with class teachers, on a termly basis. This provides a lower pupil-teacher ratio and gives ongoing in- service training for the class teacher.

Just over half of all primary and secondary schools report they add resources from their own budget to that allocated by the LEA for pupils with SEN. This usually takes the form of additional part-time non-teaching staff, and occasionally part-time teaching staff.

In reality, very few primary or secondary schools are in a position to report accurately the exact amount of funding available and used for SEN, and in consequence monitoring of the use of resources is difficult. An analysis of the resources within the schools indicates that the true cost is higher than the school estimated. This indicates an urgent need for schools to undertake a thorough audit of their provision.

The key features of school systems for the structures and deployment of resources that raise achievements of SEN pupils are:

- qualified and experienced co-ordinators who are committed and realistic about what can be achieved;

- clear job descriptions for the co-ordinator and for all other teaching and non-teaching staff;
- provision for SEN set within the context of the SDP, budgeted and costed effectively;
- accommodation and resources for SEN taken into account within whole-school planning and organisation;
- an accurate audit of need within a school which ensures the effective deployment of resources.

Monitoring

Despite the growing recognition of SEN at the planning stage, less than half of schools had appropriate monitoring procedures in place and one-quarter of schools had no monitoring in place at all.

Recognition of the importance of monitoring and evaluating provision, particularly in relation to the progress made by pupils with SEN, is more evident in schools visited in the second half of the survey period.

SENCOs frequently express frustration as they see the need to monitor and evaluate, but feel they have too little time or lack the skills to engage in a thorough process.

Key features of monitoring procedures which evaluate the provision and progress of pupils with SEN are:

- a good policy implemented consistently across a school which includes precise evaluation and monitoring arrangements;
- a consistent and systematic assessment and recording process;
- records used to inform planning and feedback to pupils and parents;
- pupils' views of their own progress or difficulties taken into account and used to inform developments;

- regular joint meetings and review to discuss progress between SENCO, class/subject teacher, and other support staff;
- planned time available for SENCO and/or SMT to observe pupils in a classroom situation;
- the interest, support and oversight by the designatedgovernor for SEN to provide an additional view of the success of policy and provision;
- the involvement of parents as partners in the learning process.

Staff development

In almost all primary schools liaison between teachers, SSAs, learning support services (LSS) and parents is sound or better, and in over half it is good; in secondary schools more difficulties arise in maintaining effective liaison, although half have good links with supporting agencies and parents. Schools realise the importance of effective joint planning and liaison between teachers, support staff and other services. This contributes to staff development.

Almost all primary and secondary schools undertake some staff development activity related to SEN. The range and quality are variable, however, from as little as a single staff meeting outlining the principles of the Code of Practice to well planned, co-ordinated, integrated programmes across a range of curricular, organisational and administrative issues that incorporate SEN.

The emphasis on training for implementation of the Code of Practice is widespread. There is a tendency to direct much of this training on the administrative detail and procedures with insufficient planning to incorporate the practicalities of teaching and learning for a diverse range of needs.

Whilst most schools have undertaken some form of recent INSET for SEN, over half requested more. This is particularly pertinent for primary SENCOs when less than half in the survey have any form of specialist SEN qualification. This rises to two-thirds of SENCOs in secondary schools having specialist training, expertise or qualification, but they, too, request more staff development.

Just over half the secondary and primary schools are providing good staff development opportunities with appropriate targets and timescales.

Key features of staff development policies and practice which help to raise the achievement of pupils with SEN are:

- priorities for the individual and the school built into the SDP and budgeted appropriately;
- liaison between the staff development co-ordinator and the SENCO to ensure funding routes and INSET activities are known and used effectively;
- in-house, regional or LEA opportunities available for all staff;
- school arrangements between local primary and secondary SENCOs to provide regular INSET and improve transitional arrangements for pupils moving between schools;
- recognition of skills held by teachers or support staff in school and locally, used to disseminate knowledge and experience of SEN issues.

6 LEA Provision

Policies and guidance, including identification and assessment

Nearly all LEAs have policies for SEN in place and the majority of these provide appropriate information and guidance for schools. Most of the survey LEAs are reviewing their policies in the light of the Code of Practice to further update and improve them with particular reference to deployment of resources and guidance on identification and assessment strategies.

It is usual to find that when the most senior staff in an LEA contribute to the formulation of the SEN policy and guidance, it is more likely to be embedded within the overall policies for an LEA. There is also a greater commitment to the implementation of policy if extensive consultation has taken place during the course of its development. The best policies are a result of consultation between headteachers, staff in schools, LSSs, voluntary organisations, parents, health and social services. Where the policy and guidance clearly detail the framework for the allocation of resources to schools for all pupils with SEN, the facility for monitoring the cost effectiveness of resourcing is more likely to be in place.

The key features of LEA policy and guidance which support schools in promoting high achievement of pupils with SEN are that they:

- articulate the principles on which the policy is based, including a summary of the range of provision for meeting the needs of pupils with SEN;
- give precise guidance to schools on identification and assessment;
- help define the target population by setting criteria for the stages which reflect the Code of Practice guidance;
- explain how access and entitlement to the curriculum may be facilitated;
- recognise and stress the importance of a partnership approach in meeting individual needs and how to develop this between: parents, pupils, school staff, governors, the LEA, health authority, social services, and the wider community;
- detail how resources are deployed;

- provide names and addresses of appropriate LEA persons with responsibilities for SEN and voluntary organisations concerned with SEN;
- establish and make clear the monitoring role of the LEA with regard to resource allocation and implementation of the policy.

Structures

Information about structure and reorganisation was obtained from the proformas returned from 28 LEAs. Since 1991, 22 had undergone one or more major reorganisations of SEN provision; three had undergone part reorganisation and three had remained stable. Twenty-four LEAs had one or more inspectors/advisers for SEN and maintained some form of LSS.

A small proportion of survey LEAs had secured a clear structure for provision for SEN over an identifiable time- scale. This enabled schools and learning support teachers to work more closely together to identify and provide for the needs of pupils across schools in the LEA.

Just over three-quarters of the LEAs had effective structures in place to provide and give support to schools. This usually includes the maintenance of some form of LSS (irrespective of how it is funded).

The key features of those LEA structures which support schools more effectively in raising the achievement of pupils with SEN are:

- specific responsibilities for SEN at senior officer level with commitment to SEN from LEA personnel;
- access by Head of Service (if a LSS exists) to policy planning meetings with LEA officers or inspectors;
- a mechanism to ensure close liaison with all providers of a service ie. Educational Psychologists, Visual and Hearing Impaired Service, Pre-School, Behavioural and

Learning Support Services;

- a career structure of permanent, full-time staff employed at differing levels, including non-teaching personnel, clear job descriptions and facility for staff development.

Deployment of resources and monitoring

Twenty-six LEAs provided information about resources for SEN. In 15 LEAs resources had increased or remained stable, and in 11 LEAs they had declined over a period of three years.

Just under half of the LEAs have criteria for the deployment or allocation of resources directly to schools or through the LSS. A similar number have efficient monitoring procedures. Without explicit criteria for allocation of resources, LEAs find it difficult to establish efficient monitoring procedures.

LEAs' preoccupation with reorganisation of SEN provision in response to recent legislation has left little time to review the quality of that provision. The few LEAs who have experienced a period of stability and included SEN within the whole educational provision have provided a cost effective service which takes account of parental choice and helps to ensure regular monitoring.

It is clear from the extreme variability of provision and practice across and within LEAs, and from the inconsistencies in the identification of pupils with SEN, that the development of criteria at LEA level for accurate identification of SEN and the equitable deployment of resources are required. Some LEAs are at last beginning to address this issue.

Key features of effective LEA systems for the initial identification of SEN and the subsequent deployment of resources are:

- the accurate knowledge of all pupils with SEN both with and without statements;
- explicit criteria and guidance to schools to ensure consistent internal assessment of pupil need - agreed between

the schools and the LEA;

- common formats for ongoing assessment, recording and monitoring of progress that informs teachers, parents, pupils, and governors of the level of need at any particular time;
- that initiatives for the review of the internal school arrangements remain the responsibility of the schools, with overall monitoring by the LEA;
- monitoring of assessment arrangements is validated by an external moderator.

Three LEA case studies demonstrate the variability in practice. Despite the inconsistencies in the way many LEAs delegate resources, common factors can be determined in almost half the LEAs that relate to higher achievement for pupils with SEN.

Large shire county

This includes an area of isolated rural communities and disadvantaged innercity.

The curricular and financial responsibility for pupils with statements is delegated to schools through a five tier banding system of cash value according to level of SEN. For pupils at Stages 1 and 2 of the Code of Practice, resources are delegated through 5 per cent of the age-weighted pupil unit and through 50 per cent compensatory awards which relate to socio-economic factors agreed through the LMS formula. For pupils at Stage 3, the resources are directed to schools via LSS level agreements. The objective is to ensure consistency and fairness in resource allocation across diverse localities.

The system is comparatively new and in the primary and secondary schools visited is working because it provides:

- *a point of reference for governors, advisers, educational psychologists, officers, parents and teachers as to the level of need in any one school through accurate identification which relies on a combination of strategies;*

- *the facility to deploy support services to objectively identified and agreed need - at Stage 3 on the SEN register;*
- *an ongoing facility to develop responsive funding arrangements in accordance with changing needs as pupils are either removed from the SEN register, require additional support or move into a new school;*
- *knowledge within the LEA about number of pupils at different stages of the SEN continuum;*
- *an efficient system that lends itself to monitoring by teachers, the SENCO, the responsible governor and the LEA itself. Moreover, it ensures that schools have a clear role and responsibility for meeting the needs of their pupils.*

Small inner London borough

Resources for pupils without a statement are delegated through the LMS formula. The LEA works in collaboration with schools to identify pupils who are placed in two broad bands which approximate to Stages 2 and 3 of the Code of Practice. Additional funding for these pupils is added to schools budgets on a pro-rata basis. Funding for pupils with a statement is centrally held and support allocated to schools through a range of LEA support services, including Educational Psychology (EP). An annual audit of provision and outcomes for pupils with SEN takes place and quality assurance procedures include an external independent evaluation. The value of this system provides:

- *an incentive to review internal school arrangements and develop good practice because of external monitoring;*
- *information to parents, teachers, schools and governors about pupils' progress;*

- *recognition in schools that the allocation of resources is fair;*
- *a raised profile of SEN in schools;*
- *consultation between officers and practitioners;*
- *a more accurate overview for the LEA of pupils with SEN and helps long term planning for those who may eventually require a statement.*

Culturally diverse small metropolitan borough

For many years the LEA has had a strong policy for integration. The policy has been to provide support to schools without using statements of SEN, through an established mainstream strategy well known and used in schools and supported by the LSS and the EP. The LEA is one of the few which has not undergone a major reorganisation of SEN provision and continues to retain all resources centrally. The strategy has been preventative; the number of statements are low as schools have had access to advice and support at an early stage. Those pupils with a statement have additional resources deployed to the school agreed by a SEN panel, and their use is monitored by the LEA.

The LSS do not work with individual children but each LSS teacher is designated a number of schools in a particular area and works with the EP to provide advice, support and help in preparing IEPs. Support is given by establishing contracts and setting specific targets for pupils. External validation of the quality of the service was commissioned as part of quality assurance. This system is working because the LEA has developed and maintained a central LSS team of highly qualified and experienced teachers. Historically the team has had a good reputation in schools, and the structures have been stable enough for consolidation of practice to develop.

This system is effective because it:

- *provides regular, external high quality SEN support to*

teachers;

- *promotes the concept that SEN is the responsibility of the school and teacher;*
- *focuses on curricular and organisational practice to alleviate SEN;*
- *undertakes ongoing assessment and internal monitoring of pupil progress by the school;*
- *promotes the notion of early intervention and the need for subsequent continuity of provision;*
- *provides high quality in-service training for class/subject teachers, SENCOs, governors and non-teaching staff.*

Staff development

Staff development was considered from two aspects. That provided by the LEA through a LSS (or other title) for teachers and non-teaching staff in schools; that provided for the LSS staff themselves.

The first aspect is that provided by LEAs for schools. The majority of LEAs in the survey are providing staff development opportunities for teaching and non-teaching staff in schools. During the survey much of the INSET was focused on the Code of Practice. The concentration of INSET to implement the Code of Practice has raised awareness of issues related to SEN, particularly regarding assessment and identification.

However, in order to raise standards for pupils with SEN it is clear from the survey that teachers need to feel confident that what they plan, teach and evaluate does meet the needs of all learners in their classes. Many teachers do not have this confidence. Practical INSET on teaching and learning strategies is said to be required. Given the increasing numbers of pupils with SEN in mainstream classes and the decreasing numbers of specialist courses available in higher education it is vital that LEAs look carefully at the training opportunities they provide in relation to the level of demand in their own particular context.

The key features of effective staff development for SEN provided by LEAs for schools are:

- an awareness and understanding of ways to access funding for SEN by key personnel in the LEA;
- an LEA staff development strategy, communicated to teachers and non-teaching support staff;
- LEA priorities which reflect schools' identified needs;
- a published INSET programme which incorporates the identified priorities;
- LEA collaboration with local higher education establishments to provide and accredit INSET activities at a variety of levels;
- high quality specialist providers;
- regular evaluation of the appropriateness and success of the training by the LEA.

The second aspect is that staff development which is provided for LSS staff. Less than half the LEAs in the survey provide appropriate training for these staff. There are two main reasons for this: LSS staff are engaged in training teachers and non-teaching staff in schools and time is not preserved for their own needs; secondly, service level agreements quite properly are beginning to target the LSS staff in school, but this reduces time for their own professional development during school days. Constant reorganisation of the majority of LSSs may have deflected the need to train their own staff on to more pressing areas of consolidation and development. Many LSS budgets do not include adequate finances for training. Often, school-based LSS staff join in with their identified schools INSET programme while this may be a strength it does not always enhance their specialist skills. The findings in Section 4 of this report clearly demonstrate that professional development is essential if high standards for pupils with SEN are to be maintained.

In the minority of LEAs where INSET provision contributes effectively to the professional development of LSS staff, the key features are:

- a well managed and co-ordinated LSS with a person responsible for staff development;
- a stated commitment and intention to regularly train staff and improve the specialist skills;
- a LSS development plan that prioritises staff development needs and is appropriately financed;
- a safeguard on the LSS staff's entitlement to five training days;
- co-operation with local higher education establishments to offer a variety of INSET opportunities that can lead to accreditation at certificate, diploma, or degree level, thus increasing specialist knowledge.

Appendix

Local Education Authorities visited in the survey

Brent
Calderdale
Cheshire
Cleveland
Coventry
Cornwall
Cumbria
Devon
Dudley
Durham
Ealing
Enfield
Essex
Gateshead
Hammersmith and Fulham
Hertfordshire
Humberside
Lambeth
Lancashire
Lincolnshire
Newham
Nottingham
Oldham
Rotherham
Shropshire
Solihull
Staffordshire
Suffolk
Sunderland
Sutton
Tameside
Tower Hamlets
Wiltshire

Printed in the United Kingdom for HMSO
Dd 301915 C20 1/96 2361 76937